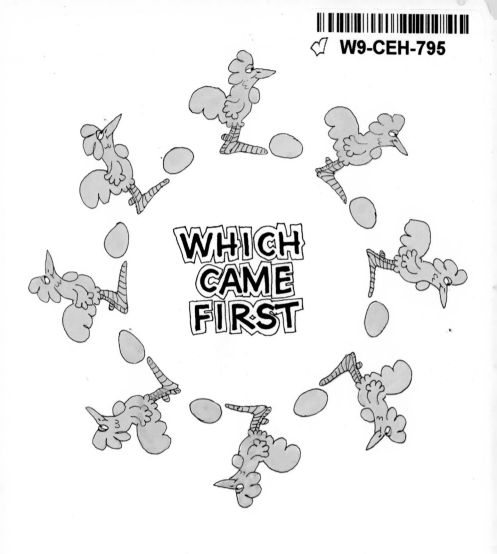

WHICH CAME FIRST

In the beginning
God said:
"Let there be
Chicken!"

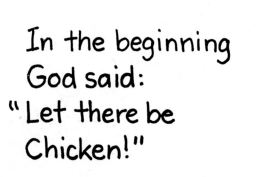

And there was
Chicken...

And God saw
it was good . . .

Finger lickin' good!

Written and conceived by Susan E. Meyer

WHICH CAME

Illustrated by Walt Lee

nd Marsha Melnick

FIRST

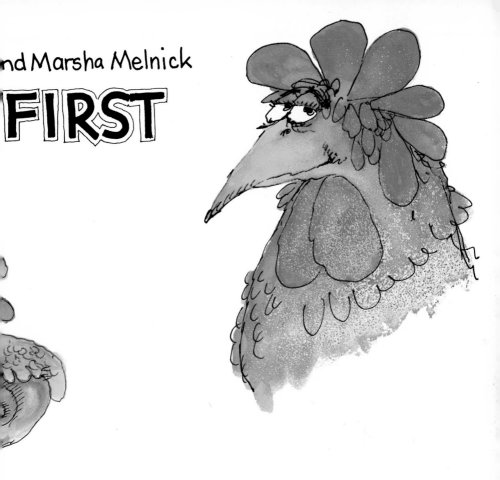

Stewart, Tabori and Chang, Publishers,
New York

Text
copyright © 1982 Roundtable Press, Inc.

Illustrations copyright © 1982 Walt Lee

Library of Congress Cataloging in Publication Data
Meyer, Susan E.
    Which came first.
        1. Chickens-Anecdotes, facetiae, satire, etc.
2. Chickens-Caricature and cartoons. I. Melnick, Marsha, II. Lee, Walt. III. Title.
PN6231.C29M4   818'.5402   82-678
ISBN 0-941434-03-6   AACR2

CONTENTS

INTRODUCTORY ADDRESS

CHICKEN SLANGUAGE AND LORE:
Chicks!, My little chickadee, Spring chicken, Don't count your chickens, Chicken Little, Chicken pox, Chicken!, Chickapoo, Chickopee, Chic....ago, Chicanery, Henpecked, Fowl play, Dumb cluck, Chicken crossing the road

OUTSTANDING CHICKEN FACTS AND FIGURES
The largest egg, The most yolks, The most eggs, Wierdo, The chicken population, The longest Flight, Bozo Miller

HOW TO RAISE 'EM, COOK 'EM, 'N, EAT 'EM:
Chicken farming, Chicken soups, Chicken fricassee, Chicken cacciatore, Roast chicken, Chicken in a basket, Arroz con pollo, Creamed chicken, Chicken flambée, Chicken teriyaki, Coq au Vin, Chicken-of-the-sea, Stuffed chicken, Minute egg waltz

FAVORITE CHICKEN PARTS:
Chicken breast, Chicken livers, Chicken fat, Chicken wings, Chicken feet, Plucked chicken, Chicken feathers

WORLD RENOWNED CHICKENS:
Liberachick, Henny Youngman, Marc Chigall, Wicked chick of the West, Atilla the Hen Moby Chick **FOWL MATTER:**

INTRODUCTORY ADDRESS

All chickens are created equal,
graceful, intelligent, colorful,
quick-witted, versatile, trust-
worthy, handsome, delicious, wise,
nimble, courageous, inexpensive

Chicks!

My little chickadee

Spring chicken

Don't count your chickens
before they hatch.

"Chicken Little, Chicken Little,
The sky is falling,
The sky is falling!"

Chicken pox

Chicken!

Chic.

.ago

Fowl play

Chicanery

Henpecked

Dumb cluck

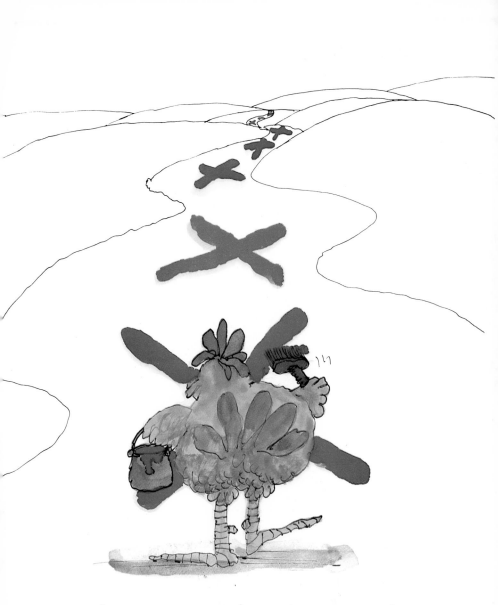

Chicken crossing the road . . .

The chicken
that didn't
make it
across the road.

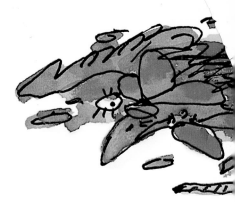

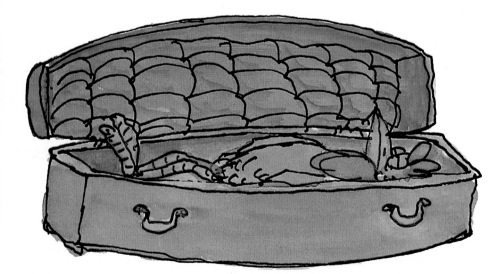

Chicken in a casket

OUTSTANDING CHICKEN FACTS AND FIGURES

Fact 1. The largest chicken egg on record was nearly 12 oz., measuring 12¼" around the long axis and 9" around the short.

Fact 3. The record for laying the most eggs: seven in one day.

Fact 2. The greatest number of yolks in one chicken egg is nine.

Fact 4. A 22 lb. rooster named Wierdo was so ferocious he slaughtered cats, maimed dogs, and reduced his rivals to chicken feed.

Fact 5. There are more chickens in the world than any other domesticated bird. More than one chicken for every human on the face of this earth.

Fact 6. The longest distance flown by any chicken is 310½ feet. (as the crow flies)

Fact 7. "Bozo" Miller from Oakland, Calif. holds the record for consuming the largest number of chickens: 27 two-pound pullets at one sitting.

HOW TO
RAISE 'EM
COOK 'EM
'N
EAT 'EM

CHICKEN FARMING

1. Egg planting (early spring)

3. Combs and eyes (end of June)

2. Sprouting of combs (around mid-May)

4. Full heads: worm feeding starts (July)

5. Half body blooms (end of August)

7. Harvesting: "Pulling Pullets" (End of September)

6. Full bodies now self-fertilizing (September)

8. A good batch of freshly pulled chickens

Monday: Chicken Noodle Soup

Tuesday:

Wednesday: Chicken Soup with Rice

Chicken Stock

Thursday: Chicken Soup
without Matzoh Balls

Friday: Chicken Fricassee

Chicken Cacciatore

Roast Chicken

Chicken
in a basket

Chicken Flambée

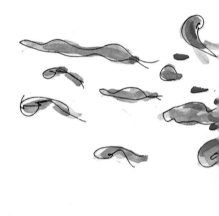

Creamed Chicken

Arroz con pollo

Chicken Teriyaki

Coq au Vin

Chicken-of-the-Sea

Stuffed Chicken

Minute Egg Waltz

Chicken breasts

Chicken livers

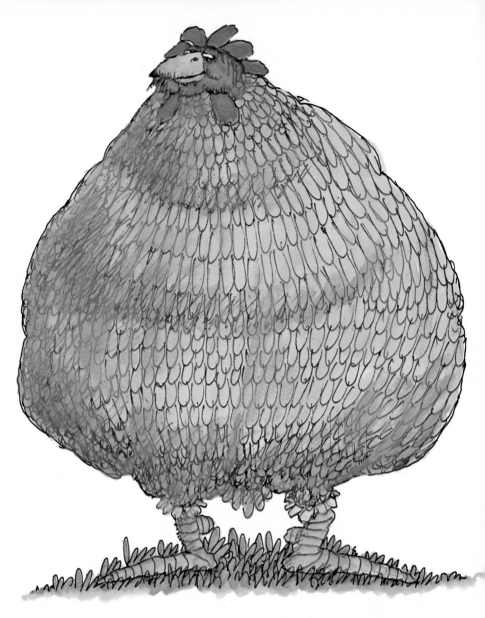

Chicken fat

Chicken wings

Chicken feet,
noses and ears

Plucked chicken

Chicken feathers.

Liberachick

Henny
Youngman

Marc Chickall

Wicked Chick of the West

Attila the Hen

Moby Chick